Snowy Owls

By Roman Patrick

Gareth Stevens
Publishing

Please visit our Web site, www.garethstevens.com. For a free color catalog of all our high-quality books, call toll free 1-800-542-2595 or fax 1-877-542-2596.

Library of Congress Cataloging-in-Publication Data

Patrick, Roman.
  Snowy owls / Roman Patrick.
      p. cm. – (Animals that live in the tundra)
  Includes index.
  ISBN 978-1-4339-3909-9 (pbk.)
  ISBN 978-1-4339-3910-5 (6-pack)
  ISBN 978-1-4339-3908-2 (library binding)
  1. Snowy owl–Juvenile literature. I. Title.
  QL696.S83P38 2011
  598.9'7–dc22

                                        2010007166

First Edition

Published in 2011 by
Gareth Stevens Publishing
111 East 14th Street, Suite 349
New York, NY 10003

Designer: Michael J. Flynn
Editor: Therese Shea

Photo credits: Cover, pp. 1, 5, 7, 9, 13, 15, 17, 19, 21, back cover Shutterstock.com; p. 11 Thomas Kokta/The Image Bank/Getty Images.

Printed in the United States of America

CPSIA compliance information: Batch #CS10GS: For further information contact Gareth Stevens, New York, New York at 1-800-542-2595.

Table of Contents

Boldface words appear in the glossary.

White as Snow

Can you guess the name of this owl? It is called a snowy owl because it is as white as snow. Snowy owls live in the **tundra** near the Arctic Ocean.

Snowy owls are not always white. Young owls have lots of brown feathers. **Males** get whiter as they get older. However, **females** never become all white.

female

male

Hunters of the Sky

Snowy owls don't mind the cold. A snowy owl has lots of feathers that cover its beak, legs, and feet. The feathers keep it warm in the tundra.

beak

legs

feet

9

Snowy owls can see very well. They hunt small animals, such as **lemmings**, mice, rabbits, birds, and fish. Sometimes, they fly south to find food.

Snowy owls have excellent hearing. This owl can hear an animal moving under the snow. The owl swoops down and uses its **talons** to catch the animal.

talons

Most owls hunt at night. Snowy owls hunt both night and day. They watch and listen for animals from tree branches. They also wait on the ground.

Mates and Babies

A snowy owl has one **mate** during its life. To find a mate, males hoot. They also bow their bodies and lift their tails.

Mother snowy owls make nests on the ground. They lay 3 to 11 eggs at a time. If there is not a lot of food, a snowy owl may not lay eggs at all.

About 1 month after the eggs are laid, baby snowy owls are born. At first, they have white feathers. Then, they get brown feathers. They become whiter as they get older.

Fast Facts

Height	up to 28 inches (71 centimeters)
Wingspan	up to 4.8 feet (1.5 meters)
Weight	up to 6.5 pounds (3 kilograms)
Diet	small animals, such as lemmings, mice, rabbits, birds, and fish
Average life span	about 10 years in the wild

Glossary

female: a girl

lemming: a small animal with a thick furry body that lives in cold northern areas

male: a boy

mate: one of a pair of animals that come together to make a baby

talon: a hooked claw

tundra: flat, treeless plain with ground that is always frozen

For More Information

Books

Ford, Ansley Watson, and Denver W. Holt. *Snowy Owls: Whoo Are They?* Missoula, MT: Mountain Press Publishing, 2008.

Frost, Helen. *Snowy Owls.* Mankato, MN: Capstone Press, 2007.

Landau, Elaine. *Snowy Owls: Hunters of the Snow and Ice.* Berkeley Heights, NJ: Enslow Publishing, 2011.

Web Sites

All About Birds: Snowy Owl
www.allaboutbirds.org/guide/Snowy_Owl/lifehistory
Hear the hoot of a snowy owl and learn more about the owl's Arctic life.

Snowy Owls
kids.nationalgeographic.com/Animals/CreatureFeature/Snowy-owl
Read facts and see a video of a snowy owl hunting in the tundra.

Index

About the Author

Roman Patrick is the writer of several children's books. He was born near the Arctic Circle and grew up loving the animals that lived there. He now lives in Buffalo, New York.